Behrouz Boochani

A Letter from Manus Island

Behrouz Boochani
A Letter from Manus Island

With a Preface by Ruth Skilbeck

A catalogue record for this
book is available from the
National Library of Australia

ISBN: 9780648398394 (pbk)

Designed and typeset by Ruth Skilbeck in Adobe
Garamond Pro 12/15

Contents

Preface

The unfolding story of exiled writer Behrouz Boochani's courage, leadership and love of humanity in an age of global disruption

Since August 2013, author, filmmaker, poet and journalist, Behrouz Boochani, has been held on Manus Island as a stateless refugee, where he has been writing, often fourteen hours a day, on his life's experiences. His articles are published in *The Guardian*, and other newspapers and periodicals around the world; and his extraordinary poetic autobiographical novel *No Friend But The Mountains*, which he wrote in text messages in Farsi (Persian) on his mobile phone, and transmitted to his translator Omid Tofighian (at the University of Sydney), was published in English in July 2018 by the global publisher Pan Macmillan. It follows the release last year of his documentary film, *Chauka Please Tell us the Time,* made from footage shot on his mobile phone at Manus Island refugee processing centre, or prison. His manifesto, *A Letter from Manus Island,* was published by *The Saturday Paper* in Australia, on 9 December 2017, and I feel privileged to have Behrouz's permission to publish his profound and significant work.

Boochani is 34, an ethnic Kurd from Ilam city, with a Master of Arts degree in Political Geography and Geopolitics from Tabiat Modares University in Tehran. Behrouz was incarcerated on Manus Island, an island of Papua New Guinea, five years ago after he fled Tehran, as an exiled journalist, to avoid arrest and imprisonment and possibly save his life, following intimidation by the authorities; due to his co-founding and editing of a political and social magazine *Werya* (or *Varia*) advocating for Kurdish language and culture. The Kurdish people are stateless and form the biggest group of stateless people in the world, and are suppressed in Iran.

Boochani had begun his career as a journalist writing for the student newspaper when he was studying at University. He freelanced for newspapers and the Iranian Sports Agency. It was when he co-founded and edited *Werya*, that he became known to the authorities.

He said in an interview as reported in the Guardian newspaper that they started it because: "The new generation are talking with their children in Farsi language and the Kurdish language and culture will be destroyed in the near future."*

Boochani was a member of the Kurdish Democratic Party which is outlawed in Iran. In 2011 he was arrested and interrogated by the paramilitary intelligence agency Sepah or the Army of the Guardians of the Islamic Revolution, and was warned to stop writing or he would be imprisoned. In 2013 the offices of *Werya* were raided by Sepah who arrested eleven of his colleagues. Boochani escaped arrest by chance as he was in Tehran. Whilst his colleagues were in jail he published an article about their arrest on the website *Iranian Reporters,* which received global attention. This put him at risk of arrest and he had to go into hiding. When two of his colleagues were released, they told him the article he wrote, and the publicity it brought, saved their lives. Sepah had been asking questions about him and they wanted to arrest him.

After travelling through southeast Asia, Boochani was ferried by business people to Christmas Island, which is Australian. The boat arrived in Australian waters just as the law was changed in 2013; instead of sailing to Australia he was sent to an "offshore processing centre" on Manus Island where he has been in limbo ever since. The law that was passed in mid 2013 forbids any 'irregular arrivals' of refugees, no matter how valid their cases. However this is in contravention of international refugee law to which Australia is a signatory, and has been the subject of ongoing controversy and contestation, since 2013, with the refugees on the Australian-run detention centre on the tiny island of Manus, left stranded in limbo for years.

For years now, Behrouz has been publishing on social media and in newspapers a stream of reports, and eloquent poetic, wrenching accounts of what it feels like to be held in this system. There have been murders at the prison camp, and suicides, and the system has been described by United Nations and Amnesty representatives, and by many who have worked there, as a form of systematic torture. He has been subjected to traumatic loss. His friends have been killed, and murdered. Reza Barati was brutally murdered by Australian-run camp guards (locals and reportedly expats who were never tried); other friends of his have been killed. In 2017 the Papua New Guinea government ordered and enforced the closure of the illegal Australian-run camps (which were run by private companies paid too much by the Australian Liberal government, audits revealed).** A proposed arrangement of 'refugee swap' with the USA, for those found to be genuine refugees to be sent to live in the USA, and refugees in the US sent to Australia in return, made almost two years ago, appears to have fallen through in the changeover to the Trump presidency, with only a few refugees flown to the USA, and Behrouz Boochani, among many hundreds, still left on the island.

I met Behrouz Boochani on Facebook. I was moved and saddened by his wrenching first hand reports in posts of what was happening in the detention camp, raw reportage that was then published in his articles in the national and international newspapers. Since 2007 I had been writing about exiled and imprisoned journalists and writers, I had interviewed writers and journalists who had been held for years in detention centres; and had published the articles in journals, and the media; research into trauma, courage and bearing witness in writing, by writers in modernity, and fugal modalities of writing that I had begun. I was publishing my book *The Writer's Fugue* and editing *Escape Artist*s anthology and I sent Behrouz a message asking if I could include a couple of his posts in my book, and if he would like to contribute to the anthology.

A Letter from Manus Island was written by Behrouz Boochani after a three week protest by the men in the camp who were refusing to leave after the illegal camp was being closed. In it, he writes of the motivations of this resistance, and what it meant in a deeply profound way.

A Letter from Manus Island is being published in *Arts Features International Issue 1, Winter 2018 'Escape Artists Anthology'*, with works by authors and artists from around the world. In his manifesto Behrouz writes of a feeling of immanence, or becoming, of feelings of profound humanity in the resisting community of refugees. He bears witness to a horrendous situation. He speaks truth to power. And from the horror, writes profound and eloquent testimonies to the beauty and dignity of the spirit of humanity which inspire respect, empathy and friendship, from which we can only learn. What would you do in his situation? Stateless and marooned. Nowhere to go. A writer, who persisted in telling and showing the world what is happening in a place where no one would want to be themselves, in a prison camp, subjected to the power of a government of a country you will never go to (and after all this who would want to?) And not only what is happening, but how it feels, in a time when journalists were banned. His courage is admirable, and astonishing.

Read and re-read his manifesto in *A Letter from Manus Island*, and be inspired by the wisdom in his words, in what he describes. For what he talks of is, as he says, what all humans need, in an era of increasing global disruption and automated robotic systems which are alienating, and dehumanising; we need to remember and feel our humanity, what differentiates us from machines, and we need to experience friendship, compassion, companionship, justice and love. All things that the men experienced in their peaceful protest against a violent governmentality, he writes in his humanitarian message.

Take inspiration and courage from his words.

Ruth Skilbeck, August 2018

Notes

* See Ben Doherty, 'Day of the Imprisoned Writer: Behrouz Boochani—detained on Manus Island,' *The Guardian*, Nov. 15, 2015.
**See Ruth Skilbeck, *The Writer's Fugue: Musicalization, Trauma and Subjectivity in the Literature of Modernity* second edition; third edition, 2017; 2018, pp. 65-68

Behrouz Boochani
A Letter from Manus Island

"Here is the Manus resistance manifesto I have written based on my experiences over the past months. I would like to invite Australian society to read this piece. I wrote it in a way to wake Australia up. #Manus."

Behrouz Boochani, Twitter, 7 December, 2017

For many months, the refugees living inside Manus prison have had to endure extraordinarily oppressive conditions orchestrated by the Australian government. During this time, the Department of Immigration used various strategies in order to force refugees out and transfer them into three new camps: East Lorengau, Hillside and West Haus.

They announced October 31 as the deadline for refugees to leave the place.

That date signalled the beginning of extreme force and dictatorship. The government believed October 31 would be the date its vision would become a reality and its plans would be put into practice. When this date arrived, 600 refugees refused to transfer to the new camps. Instead, the situation transformed into a humanitarian crisis that lasted 22 days.

For many watching the events on the island and in the prison from the outside, some central questions have arisen. How could we continue resisting without food, water and medicine for three weeks? How did we keep the character of our protest peaceful throughout this period? How did we continue resisting without ever resorting to violence?

From the standpoint of someone operating at the core of the resistance for this long period of time – that is, the whole three-week period – and privy to everything that was happening inside the prison and the details of the resistance, I think the only thing that helped us persevere for the long stretch of time was our dedication to principles of humanity and human values.

In the community meetings we held every day at 5pm, we

stayed true to the principles of love, friendship and brotherhood.

There was nothing greater for us than respect. There was nothing greater for us than equality and camaraderie.

We have reminded a majority of the Australian public that throughout their history they have only ever imagined that their democracy and freedom has been created on the basis of principles of humanity.

In reality, it was a resistance that was completely democratic. By democratic I mean that every day, right at 5pm, at one fixed location in Delta prison, we gathered and everyone had the chance to express their opinion with the group and discuss. If anyone had a new suggestion, they could outline it and then we would put it to a vote; as a group we would consider whether the suggestion should be put into practice or not.

Debates surrounding how to manage the tasks inside the prison and the rules pertaining to the prison were also resolved by voting. This was in addition to deciding on other methods we should incorporate that could help stand up to power and continue our struggle.

Throughout these three weeks, the gates were completely open and anyone could leave the collective resistance at any moment. They were totally free to go to the new camps and acquire food and water. We were particularly committed to the following point: no one had the right to reproach another for leaving us. In fact, we all had to thank anyone who left the community because they stood with us for as long as they were capable, and we were all grateful for that.

Sometimes, during this period, we smuggled into the prison a limited amount of food in the dead of night, and this food would be distributed equally among the prisoners. This principle also applied to the dogs that live among us: we factored them in. In our meetings we were adamant about the fact we had to show even more compassion to these dogs than before. Feeding them was imperative. These principles applied to the sick, too; we cared for them now more than ever before.

And so the emotional connection and collaborative work began to take shape between special groups of people in Australia, numerous local Manusians, and all of us detained here. This collective sentiment developed into an important partnership in support of our struggle. During that three-week period, special people in Australia united with many people on Manus and made attempts to deliver food inside the camp. Ultimately, this meant that the Papua New Guinea police and navy intensified their strategies as the boats carrying supplies got closer to the main prison camp.

Manusians also organised a protest in Lorengau to support us. The protesters, both in Australia and in Papua New Guinea, are not the majority, but they are representative of the conscience of their societies. They are among the people who are socially and politically aware.

In any case, these interrelations between the three communities, all with different cultures and nationalities, proved that there exist people with a sincere understanding of other people, no matter where they are in the world. It proves that there always exist significant people who transcend government ideologies.

I imagine the rallies that were organised can be nothing more than messages of friendship and humanity. But apart from these spaces of solidarity and the alliances formed between societies, the question remains: What are the conditions and the framework that give rise to a resistance constituted by half-naked men on a remote island known as Manus? And what are the messages that this resistance is attempting to convey?

The refugees are overpowered.

The refugees have had extraordinary pressure imposed on them.

The refugees have resisted an entire political system; they have stood up to the power of a whole government.

From the very beginning right through to the very end, the refugees only used peaceful means to stand up and challenge power.

The refugees have asserted their authority.

The refugees have claimed power.

The refugees were able to reimagine themselves in the face of the detention regime.

The refugees were able to re-envision their personhood when suppressed by every form of torture inflicted on them and when confronted by every application of violence.

According to its own logic, and consistent with the character it has moulded itself into, the detention regime wanted to manufacture a particular kind of refugee with a particular kind of response. However, the refugees were able to regain their identity, regain their rights, regain their dignity. In fact, what has occurred is essentially a new form of identification, which asserts that we are human beings.

The refugees have been able to reconfigure the images of themselves as passive actors and weak subjects into active agents and fierce resistors. The concept of the refugee as a passive actor was an ideal instrument in the hands of power and could be exploited by Australia's political machinations; it formed the refugees into something that could be manipulated and leveraged for the Australian government's own purpose.

The refugees have established that they desire to exist only as free individuals. They desire only an honourable existence. They have established this in confrontation with the proliferation of violence in the detention centre, one that is implemented by a mighty power structure. Up against the determination of this monolith, the refugees have, ultimately, vindicated themselves.

The refugees have been able to refashion the image of themselves as the "Other". We have reshaped the understanding of us as politically inept and have been successful in projecting an image of who we are. We now present the real face of refugees for a democratic Australia to discern.

The refugees have found the responses and reasoning provided by the government regarding the hostage situation and our incarceration to be absurd. There have been ridiculous fabrications. We have exposed this as a form of political opportunism, as a politics driven by economic mismanagement and incompetence, policies that benefit bloodthirsty financial investors, a politics that experiments in order to further ingrain a system of border militarisation and securitisation.

The refugees have identified and exposed the face of an emerging 21st-century dictatorship and fascism, a dictatorship and fascism that will one day creep into Australian society and into people's homes like a cancer.

The refugees have been resisting with their very lives.

Against the real politics of the day.

With their very bodies.

With peace as a way of being and as an expression.

With a rejection of violence.

With a kind of political poetics.

With a particular style of poetic resistance.

These features have become one with their existence.

Refugees pushed back.

Risking their lives and bodies.

Just fragile humans risking everything.

Risking everything that is beautiful.

Risking the only things of value left to them.

Risking what nature had bestowed upon them.

They never gave up these things to become mere bodies subject to politics. In opposition to a system of discipline and the mechanisation of their bodies, the detained did not surrender. In reality, they proved that the human being is not a creature that can be entirely and completely consumed by politics.

From another perspective, this mode of resistance and the

messages communicated by the imprisoned is nothing more than refugees asserting and putting into practice their values and their standpoints. They took this stance in order to return something valuable to the majority of the Australian public, to return what it has lost, or what it is in the process of losing. We formulated a schema of humanity that is, precisely, in polar opposition to fascist thinking – the kind of thinking that created Manus prison.

We have reminded a majority of the Australian public that throughout their history they have only ever imagined that their democracy and freedom has been created on the basis of principles of humanity.

If a majority of Australians were to reflect deeply on our resistance and sympathise with us, they would come to realise something about how they imagined themselves to be until now.

They would undergo a kind of self-realisation regarding their illusions of moral superiority.

And they would be forced to self-analyse in relation to the principles and values they hold dear at this point in time, and realise that they are not connected to a mythical moral past.

Our resistance is the spirit that haunts Australia. Our resistance is a new manifesto for humanity and love.

In any case, our resistance and the three weeks of hardship we endured produced a new perspective and method that was remarkably transformative, even for us incarcerated within Manus prison. We learnt that humans have no sanctuary except within other human beings. Humans have no felicitous way to live their lives other than to trust in other humans, and the hearts of other humans, and the warmth within the hearts of other humans.

Our resistance enacted a profound poetic performance. This persisted until the moment we were confronted with the extremity of the violence. We found that the baton-wielding police had killed one of the dogs we had adopted into our community. At that moment, we descended into sorrow and wept,

in honour of its loyalty,

its beauty,

its innocence.

This profound poetic performance was implemented on another occasion when we were facing off against a group of police officers. We linked our arms to create a chain and told them that we only had love for them. We recited this as a poem that then became a collective expression:

A poem that united us.

A poem that we chanted in unison.

A poem of peace.

A poem of humanity.

A poem of love.

When the police chief stood in front of the community of half-naked refugees and named the leaders over the loud-speaker, asking them to surrender themselves, everyone called out:

"I'm A ...!"

"I'm Y …!"

"I'm B …!"

This was the scene that emerged in Manus prison.

On the same day that we were brutally bashed, a number of individuals placed flowers in their hair. A sick Rohingya man put two red flowers behind his ears and smiled even as his body was emaciated and in the worst shape possible.

Our resistance was an epic of love.

In any case, I think that our resistance, our strategy of defiance, our message of protest, are the product of years of captivity, of a life of captivity, all produced by captives of a violent governmentality in Manus prison.

Resistance in its purest form.

A noble resistance.

An epic constituted by half-naked bodies up against a violent governmentality.

All this violence designed in government spaces and targeted against us has driven our lives towards nature.

towards the natural environment,

towards the animal world,

towards the ecosystem.

It has pushed us in this direction since we hope that maybe we could make its meaning, beauty and affection part of our reality. And coming to this realisation is the most pristine, compassionate and non-violent relationship and encounter possible for the imprisoned refugees in terms of rebuilding our lives and identities.

We built profound relationships with the indigenous people, with the children, with the birds, the interaction between elements of society, even with the dog that was killed under the brutality of the system.

But the prison and its violence will never accept this, and in every situation the imprisoned lives and spirits have to reconfigure themselves in the face of death; they avoid projecting the malevolent dimension of their existence as the most dominant.

Ultimately, they beat us down and with violence put an end to our peaceful protest. But I think we were able to communicate our humanitarian message to Australian society and beyond. This sentiment is what all people, whether in Australia or elsewhere, need more than anything else these days.

Feelings of friendship.

Feelings of compassion.

Feelings of companionship.

Feelings of justice.

And feelings of love.

Translation: Omid Tofighian, American University in Cairo/
University of Sydney

Acknowledgment:

Behrouz Boochani's *A Letter from Manus* was first published
by *The Saturday Paper* in December 2017. It is republished in
Arts Features International Issue 1, Winter 2018, 'Escape Artists'
and here with kind permission of Behrouz Boochani.

Borderstream Books

Out in August 2018

Arts Features International, Issue 1, Winter 2018
Escape Artists Anthology

**Arts Features
International**

Issue 1, Winter 2018

ESCAPE ARTISTS ANTHOLOGY
Edited by Ruth Skilbeck

Arts Features International, Issue 1, Winter 2018 magazine presents a global conversation in *Escape Artists Anthology*. Artists, authors, novelists, essayists, poets, playwrights, and filmmakers from around the world engage with issues of cultural and political relevance; in book extracts, letters, poetry, short stories, new work, memoir, articles, interviews, artworks and more.

312 pages
ISBN: 9780648299899 - paperback RRP $35.00 (AUD)
ISBN: 9780648245421- hardback RRP $50.00 (AUD)
ISBN: 9780648245445- ebook-pdf RRP $26.00 (AUD)
www.borderstreambooks.com.au

Borderstream Books

A Brief Guide to Middle Class Homelessness

By Kenneth Wolman

Publication year: 2017

34 pages
Paperback
ISBN: 9780648099031
RRP $20.00 (AUD)

Ebook-pdf
ISBN: 9780648245407
RRP $12.00 (AUD)

In 1987, Kenneth Wolman's critical opinion article on homelessness was published in The New York Times. Twenty-five years later he himself became homeless after marriage breakdown, and the end of his adjunct teaching and technical writing contract employment in financial services companies on Wall Street. In his critically and culturally significant literary essay, poet Kenneth Wolman, Ph.D., tells the moving story of his year in men's shelters in Paterson, New Jersey, aged 70, reflecting on his experiences in social and psychological context. His memoir is published with a preface, in a pamphlet.

.

CPSIA information can be obtained
at www.ICGtesting.com
Printed in the USA
LVHW111521080219
606906LV00001B/65/P

9 780648 398394